Date: 8/3/12

J 530.4 WAL
Walker, Sally M.
Investigating matter /

How
Does Energy
Work?

Investigating
Matter

Sally M. Walker

Lerner Publications Company
Minneapolis

Author's note: The experiments in this book use the metric measurement system, as that's the system most commonly used by scientists.

Lerner Publications Company
A division of Lerner Publishing Group, Inc.
241 First Avenue North
Minneapolis, MN 55401 U.S.A.

Website address: www.lernerbooks.com

Library of Congress Cataloging-in-Publication Data

Walker, Sally M.
        Investigating Matter / by Sally M. Walker.
            p.   cm. — (Searchlight books™—How does energy work?)
        Includes index.
        ISBN 978-0-7613-5776-6 (lib. bdg. : alk. paper)
        1. Matter—Constitution—Juvenile literature. 2. Change of state (Physics)—
Juvenile literature. I. Title.
        QC173.16.W35 2012
        530—dc22   2010040261

Manufactured in the United States of America
1 – DP – 7/15/11

Contents

Chapter 1

WHAT IS MATTER?

Everything around you is made of matter. Matter can be soft or hard. Matter can be any color. It can even be invisible.

Everything in your classroom is made of matter. What are the three states of matter?

Matter takes up space. It can be weighed. Solid objects are made of matter. So are liquids like water and gases like air. Solids, liquids, and gases are the three states of matter.

All matter takes up space and can be weighed.

Matter has mass. Mass is the amount of matter an object is made of. A lot of mass is harder to lift than a small amount of mass.

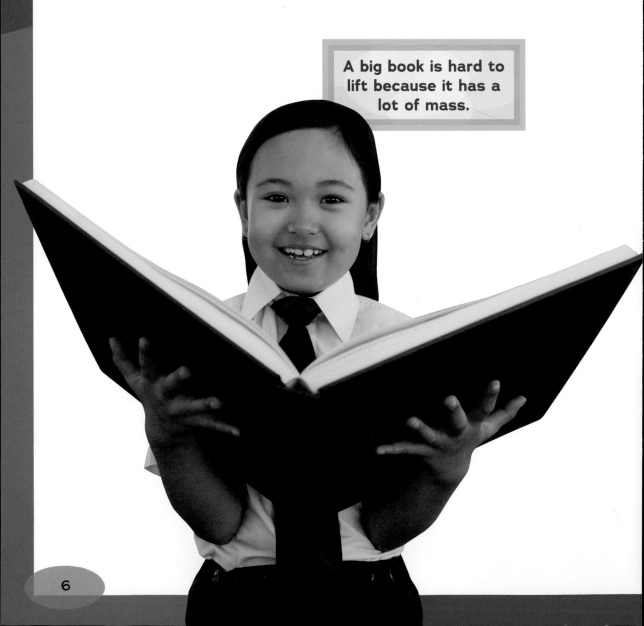

A big book is hard to lift because it has a lot of mass.

Prove It!

Find an empty jug and a water faucet. The jug looks empty. But it is filled with matter. Can you guess what the matter is? It's air. Air takes up space inside the jug. But the air doesn't have much mass. It's easy to lift the jug.

Air doesn't have much mass. A jug filled with air is easy to lift.

Fill the jug with water. The space inside the jug is the same as before. But it is much harder to lift the jug now. That's because the matter inside it has more mass. Water has much more mass than air.

Matter is made of tiny particles called atoms. Billions of atoms can fit on the period at the end of this sentence.

A jug filled with water is much harder to lift than a jug filled with air.

Atoms and Molecules

Atoms can join together to form groups called molecules. Molecules are bigger than atoms. But millions of molecules would still fit on a period.

Molecules are always moving. Some molecules have a lot of space around them. They can move freely. Other molecules are packed tightly together. They still move, but not as freely. Prove it with this experiment.

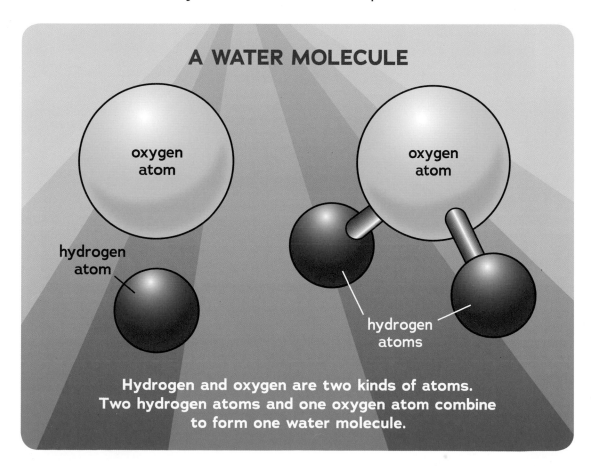

A WATER MOLECULE

oxygen atom

oxygen atom

hydrogen atom

hydrogen atoms

Hydrogen and oxygen are two kinds of atoms.
Two hydrogen atoms and one oxygen atom combine
to form one water molecule.

These kids are pretending to be molecules that have a lot of space around them. They can move without bumping into one another.

Experiment Time

Stand in a big room with two friends.

Spread your arms like airplane wings. Pretend to fly around the room. You have plenty of space. It's easy to fly without bumping into your friends. Molecules with lots of space around them don't bump into one another very often.

Put your arms at your sides. Stand as close to your friends as you can without touching. You are packed tightly together. You can't spread your arms without hitting one another. But you can still move. You can shake or jump up and down. When you all move at once, you may bump into one another. Tightly packed molecules move the same way.

If you stand very close to your friends, you can't move much without bumping into one another.

Chapter 2

TAKING UP SPACE

All matter takes up space. The amount of space that an object fills is called its volume. To find the volume of an object, you must know its length, width, and height. The volume of a solid is measured in cubic units, such as cubic inches or cubic centimeters. A cubic unit includes length, width, and height.

Matter takes up space. What do we call the amount of space that an object takes up?

A solid object's volume always stays the same. You can move the object or break it into pieces. But it still takes up the same amount of space. You can prove this. You will need twenty-seven cubes of sugar.

Sugar cubes are solid matter. Each sugar cube's volume is about 1 cubic centimeter.

Experiment Time Again

Put the cubes in a line on a table. Each cube is about 1 centimeter long. So the length of the sugar line is 27 centimeters. But this measurement doesn't tell you the sugar's volume. You need two more measurements. Can you guess what they are?

Make a long, narrow line out of the twenty-seven sugar cubes.

To find the volume, you must also know the width and height of the sugar line. The width is 1 centimeter. The height is also 1 centimeter. Now you have all the measurements you need.

First, multiply the width of the line by its height. 1 × 1 = 1. Then multiply your answer by the line's length. 1 × 27 = 27. So the volume of the long, narrow line of sugar is 27 cubic centimeters.

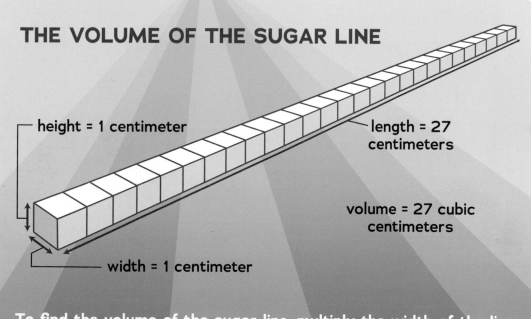

THE VOLUME OF THE SUGAR LINE

height = 1 centimeter

length = 27 centimeters

volume = 27 cubic centimeters

width = 1 centimeter

To find the volume of the sugar line, multiply the width of the line by its height. Then multiply your answer by the line's length.

Next, stack the sugar cubes. Put three cubes in each stack. You'll have nine stacks. Push the stacks together to make a giant sugar cube. The giant cube is 3 centimeters wide, 3 centimeters high, and 3 centimeters long. Does it take up the same amount of space as the long, narrow sugar line? Find the giant cube's volume and see.

Stack the 27 sugar cubes to make a giant cube. The cube will be 3 cubes wide, 3 cubes high, and 3 cubes long.

Multiply the width of the cube by its height. 3 × 3 = 9. Then multiply your answer by the cube's length. 9 × 3 = 27. The volume of the giant cube is 27 cubic centimeters.

The volume of the giant cube is exactly the same as the volume of the sugar line. The cube just looks smaller because the sugar blocks were moved around.

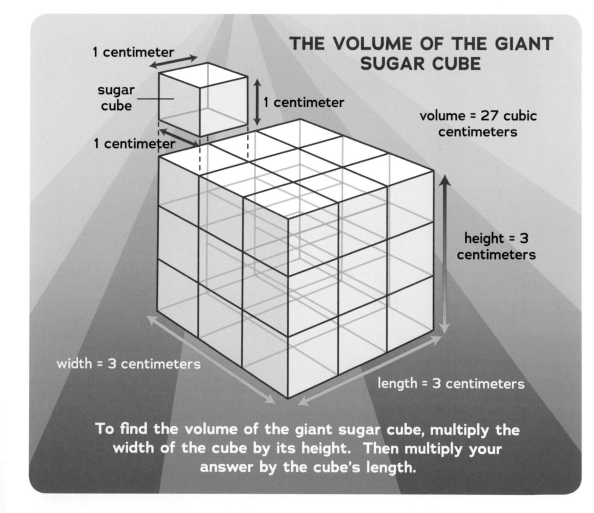

THE VOLUME OF THE GIANT SUGAR CUBE

1 centimeter

sugar cube

1 centimeter

1 centimeter

volume = 27 cubic centimeters

height = 3 centimeters

width = 3 centimeters

length = 3 centimeters

To find the volume of the giant sugar cube, multiply the width of the cube by its height. Then multiply your answer by the cube's length.

17

Chapter 3

SOLID MATTER

The shape and volume of solid matter always stay the same. Chalk is solid matter. Its molecules are arranged in a certain pattern. Chalk can be broken. But the molecules in each piece still have the same pattern.

Chalk molecules are arranged in a certain pattern. If you break a piece of chalk, does the pattern change?

Acting Like a Solid

Think about the moving molecule experiment you did. When were you more like something solid? Your group was more solid when you stood close together.

Stand close to your two friends again. Wrap your arms around one another. Your group is really packed together. Its shape can't change. The molecules in solid matter always stay in the same place. The solid keeps its shape.

THESE KIDS ARE PRETENDING TO BE MOLECULES THAT ARE PACKED TOGETHER IN SOLID MATTER.

When the molecules in matter are very close together, scientists say the matter is dense. Molecules in most solids are tightly packed. So solids are dense matter.

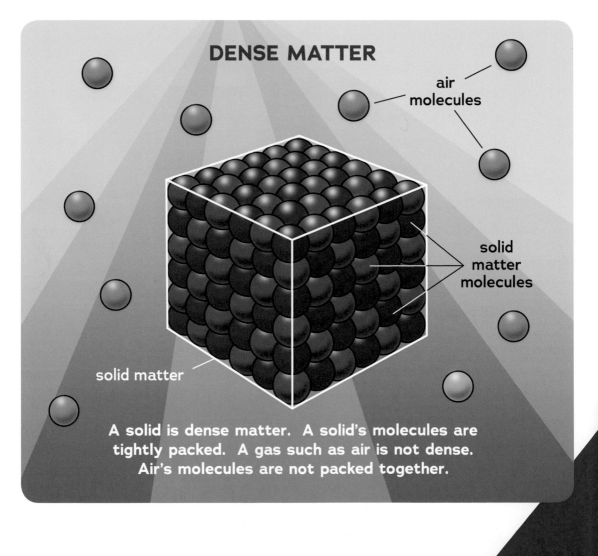

DENSE MATTER

air molecules

solid matter molecules

solid matter

A solid is dense matter. A solid's molecules are tightly packed. A gas such as air is not dense. Air's molecules are not packed together.

Chapter 4

LIQUID MATTER

Liquids are another state of matter. Liquids are usually measured in fluid ounces or milliliters. These units don't have *cubic* in their names. But they are still cubic units because they include length, width, and height.

Water is liquid matter. How would you measure water?

The volume of a solid always stays the same. So does the volume of a liquid. But liquids are very different from solids.

Try This

Fill a glass with water. Watch how the water comes out of the faucet. Does it fall out in hard chunks, like blocks from a box? No, water flows in a stream.

Solid matter stays in hard chunks. But liquid matter flows smoothly.

A liquid does not have just one shape. Pour the water from your glass into a bowl. See how the molecules quickly spread to fit the bowl's shape. A liquid flows into all parts of a container. It spreads out until its surface is smooth.

Liquid matter flows to fill the bottom of any container.

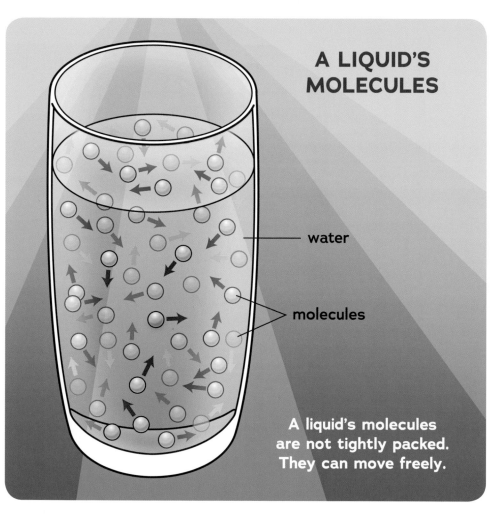

Free-Moving Molecules

You can pour a liquid because its molecules can move freely. They don't cling together as tightly as the molecules in a solid. The liquid's molecules are not as tightly packed. Liquids are less dense than solids.

Some liquids are more dense than other liquids. You can prove it. You will need a measuring cup, cooking oil, a glass, liquid soap, water, and food coloring.

EXPERIMENT WITH DIFFERENT LIQUIDS TO SEE WHICH ONE IS MORE DENSE.

When you pour the soap into the glass, it sinks to the bottom. The oil rises to the top. The soap sinks because it is denser than the oil.

Now Try This

Pour ¼ cup of oil into the glass. Then pour in ¼ cup of liquid soap. What happens to the soap? Why do you think it sinks to the bottom?

The molecules in the soap are more tightly packed than the molecules in the oil. Because the soap is more dense, it is heavier. It sinks beneath the oil.

Get ¼ cup of water. Add one drop of food coloring to it. Slowly add the colored water to the oil and soap in the glass. What happens? Is the water more dense than the oil? Is the water more dense than the soap?

THE WATER SINKS BELOW THE OIL. BUT THE WATER FLOATS ABOVE THE SOAP.

Chapter 5

MATTER AS GAS

Gases are the third state of matter. The molecules in gases are far apart. They are so far apart that we can't see them. But we know they are there. We can't see air. But we can see leaves blow in the wind. Wind is moving air.

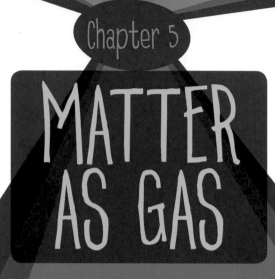

Air is a gas. Gases can't be seen. How can you tell when air is moving?

Gases are invisible. But they still take up space, just like solids and liquids. You can prove this with a drinking straw and a tiny piece of paper.

A straw looks empty. But it is filled with air.

Testing It Out

Look at the straw. Is it filled with anything? Yes, it's filled with air. Put one end of the straw in your mouth. Look up at the ceiling. Balance the tiny paper on the other end of the straw. Blow through the straw.

What happens to the paper? It blows off. Why does this happen? The air leaving your mouth needs space. It pushes the air that is already in the straw. The straw's air pushes against the paper. It pushes the paper away.

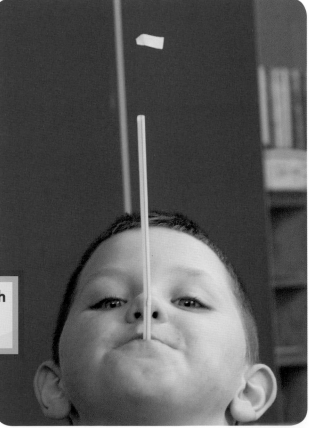

When you blow air through the straw, the air pushes the paper off the straw.

Like liquids, gases can change shape. The molecules in gases move around even more freely than the molecules in liquids. If you blow air into a glass, the air does not stay at the bottom. Instead, air molecules flow freely up and out of the glass.

When you blow air bubbles in water, the air moves up and out of the water.

To keep a gas in a container, you must completely enclose it. Blow air into a balloon. If you don't hold the balloon closed, the air rushes out. But if you tie the balloon, the gas is enclosed. The balloon stays full.

A gas spreads out to fill whatever container it is in. The air from your small balloon could spread out to fill a whole room.

To keep air in a balloon, you have to hold the balloon closed or tie its neck. Otherwise, the air rushes out.

Chapter 6

MATTER CAN CHANGE STATES

Matter can change from one state to another. Adding heat to matter makes molecules move faster. Taking away heat makes them move slower. When molecules move faster or slower, they can change state.

When ice melts, it changes from a solid state to a liquid state. What makes molecules change from one state to another?

Water: Versatile Matter

Water can be found in all three states. Solid water is called ice. When ice melts, it turns into liquid water. When liquid water evaporates, it changes into a gas.

   You can make water change its state. You will need a few ice cubes, a small pan, and a stove or a hot plate. Wear safety glasses, use a pot holder when handling the pan, and ask an adult to help you.

To make water change its state, you need a pan, a stove or a hot plate, safety glasses, and some ice cubes.

Experimenting with Water

Dump the ice cubes into the pan. Put the pan on the stove or the hot plate. Turn the burner on. What happens to the ice cubes as they are heated? They melt. The solid ice changes into liquid water.

PUT A FEW ICE CUBES INTO THE PAN. THEN TURN ON THE BURNER.

As the water heats, can you see bubbles? What do you think is inside the bubbles? Water vapor is inside them. Water vapor is water in the gas state. How do the bubbles move as the water gets hotter? They rise to the top. Soon the water's surface will be bubbling fast. This is called boiling. The gas bubbles pop and escape from the pan. They form a cloud of steam. Steam is hot water vapor.

You have made matter change its state. Your solid ice cubes changed into liquid water. Then the liquid changed into a gas.

The bubbles in boiling water are made of water vapor. The bubbles rise to the surface and pop. Then the water vapor goes up into the air.

Our world is made of matter. Everything around you is a solid, a liquid, or a gas. Even you are made of matter. Can you name any of the solids, liquids, and gases in your body? It's a question that really matters!

You take up space, and you can be weighed. So you are made of matter.

Glossary

atom: a very tiny particle that makes up all things

boiling: bubbling and changing from a liquid into a gas

cubic units: units for measuring the amount of space things fill

dense: having molecules that are very close together

evaporate: to change from a liquid into a gas

gas: a substance that can change its size and shape.   A gas can spread out to fill any container.

ice: solid water

liquid: a substance that flows easily. A liquid always stays the same size, but its shape can change.

mass: the amount of matter an object is made of

matter: what all things are made of. Matter takes up space and can be weighed.

melt: to change from a solid into a liquid

molecule: the smallest piece that a substance can be broken into. A molecule is made up of atoms that are joined together.

solid: a substance that stays the same size and shape. The molecules in most solids are tightly packed.

state: the solid, liquid, or gas form of matter

steam: hot water vapor

volume: the amount of space that an object fills

water vapor: water in the gas state

Learn More about Matter

Books

Boothroyd, Jennifer. *Many Kinds of Matter: A Look at Solids, Liquids, and Gases.* Minneapolis: Lerner Publications Company, 2011. This easy-to-read book offers a good basic review of solids, liquids, and gases.

Cook, Trevor. *Experiments with States of Matter.* New York: PowerKids Press, 2009. Check out this book to find interesting experiments related to matter.

Monroe, Tilda. *What Do You Know about States of Matter?* New York: PowerKids Press, 2011. Learn more about the three states of matter.

Mullins, Matt. *Super Cool Science Experiments: States of Matter.* Ann Arbor, MI: Cherry Lake Publishing, 2010. This title features more matter-related experiments for you to try.

Websites

BBC Bitesize Science: Changing State
http://www.bbc.co.uk/schools/ks2bitesize/science/materials/changing_state/play.shtml
Try fun virtual science experiments at this website.

Enchanted Learning: Phases of Matter
http://www.enchantedlearning.com/physics/Phasesofmatter.shtml
Read about solids, liquids, gases, and more on this informative page.

Water
http://www.nyu.edu/pages/mathmol/textbook/3gradecover.html
Find out all about water as a solid, a liquid, and a gas. Activities are included.

Index

Photo Acknowledgments

Photographs copyright © Andy King. Additional images in this book are used with the permission of: © LWA/Dann Tardif/Blend Images/Getty Images, p. 4; © Jacobs Stock Photography/Photographer's Choice RF/Getty Images, p. 6; © Laura Westlund/Independent Picture Service, pp. 9, 15, 17, 20, 24; © Michael Blann/Digital Vision/Getty Images, p. 28; © Chris Harris/All Canada Photos/Alamy, p. 33.

Front Cover: © Peter Donaldson/Alamy.

Main body text set in Adrianna Regular 14/20.
Typeface provided by Chank.